W9-BLJ-934

Acknowledgements

LIBERATING LITURGIES
Created by members of the Women's Ordination Conference

Editorial Board Members
Barbara A. Cullom
Sheila Doran-Benyon
Myriel Eykamp
Mary Frohlich
Ruth McDonough Fitzpatrick
Eileen O'Brien Merchant
Lynne Schmidt, SSND

Editorial Team
Elaine Marie Crumby Clipson
Fidelis McDonough R.S.M.
Eileen Hanrahan Queene

Editorial Coordinator
Ruth McDonough Fitzpatrick

Editorial Assistant
Theresa Anderson, OSB

Women's Ordination Conference
P. O. Box 2693
Suite #11
Fairfax Circle Center
9653 Lee Highway
Fairfax, VA 22031
Phone: (703) 352-1006
© **Copyright 1989** Permission to make copies of a ritual in whole or in part for a one-time private use for the sole purpose of facilitating community prayer is hereby granted.

Artwork: Sally Hanlon
Book and Cover Design: Center for Educational Design and Communication
Washington, D.C

Printed in The United States of America
ISBN 0-9623386-1-3

Liberating Liturgies

Women's Ordination Conference

TABLE OF CONTENTS

PRESENTATION

So many people have worked for such a long time on this collection of liturgies, that it is impossible to thank everyone, or even know who you all are, for this book is truly a grassroots collection of liturgies celebrated by WOC members over the past years.

Some names are outstanding, in that they keep cropping up in the WOC files dealing with this project: Mary Frohlich for responding to the Core Commission's suggestion to launch this project; Eileen O'Brien Merchant for animating the fledgling; Sheila Doran-Benyon, Myriel Eykamp, Lynne Schmidt, Margaret Smith and Marian Kelley for preliminary readings and structural suggestions; Fidelis McDonough and the Sisters of Mercy for picking up the floundering project and setting it on a firmer financial foundation; Elaine Clipson, Eileen Queener and Fidelis for their collective editorial process; Barbara Cullom for processing it on her Macintosh, Sally Hanlon for her art-word-work, Theresa Anderson for her precise follow-up work and Melanie Guste at the Center for Educational Design and Communication for her patient support and creative desktop publishing. Thanks to Martha Ann Kirk for her encouragement and inspiration as well as Diann Neu, who constantly gives of herself as she empowers us all to break old models and create new rituals that reflect our experiences as women-church while we struggle to become a discipleship of equals.

I would like to thank Ruby Cribbin, who early on, admonished us to: "Struggle. Struggle. Struggle. Refuse to accept the standard approach. Believe that the very process by which we approach something contains within it the values, etc. we are seeking. . . to probe more deeply and ritualize today this very probing."

Since I have been part of the process from conception to publication, I am proud to be able to say that this has been truly a collaborative endeavor, which is the way I think all liturgy should be. Thank you to all who contributed liturgies, time, energy and money to make it become a reality. We regret that not all submissions could be accepted for publication.

We were prophetic, when in 1984, we first thought of a feminist liturgy book collected from WOC members. Because of lack of money we have had to go very slowly, while other books were printed one after another. But we have maintained our integrity. Proceeds from this book will first pay the printer and then help launch a second collection. Please help publicize and spread the word about this resource.

Now that this first book is finished, are you ready to start again? Send WOC your favorite liturgies to inspire and share with others. Include a short description of the time, place and circumstances that helped create your liturgy. Clear photographs would be helpful, too. Please supply all copyright information for references used. Send us the feminist liturgies that you celebrate outside the doors of Cathedrals when our male companions are being ordained; when bishops refuse to wash female feet on Holy Thursday; the inclusive liturgies you participate in when you can no longer stand the pain of exclusive church structures; the ones that keep you in the struggle for peace and justice in Central America; liturgies that give thanks and praise to God/dess for liberation struggles and equality struggles around the world and around your neighborhood. Your Women-Church celebrations. The ones you celebrate with your communities and what you work into mainstream church life. Send us the liturgies you celebrate at priestless parishes or when the priest cannot make it to your friend's deathbed. Language will be, of course, all-inclusive and references to God, gender-free. This is not a finished product. We are in a process of struggle, of becoming a discipleship of equals. Let us go in peace to love and serve our liberating God.

Ruth McDonough Fitzpatrick
National Coordinator
Women's Ordination Conference
Fairfax, Virginia
May, 1989

INTRODUCTION

Do we have words of prayer? As the friends gathered around Jesus, we beg "Teach us to pray" and we take consolation that the Spirit is teaching us to pray. But often our prayer is inarticulate groans, groans of the pain of being battered through the ages, groans of distrusting our experiences and our words, but more and more the groans are those giving birth to a new creation.

Over 130 million more females than males in the world do not learn to read and write. If, or when these girls and women do learn, will they read stories which will empower them to claim their own wisdom and fully use their gifts? Or will they, like those of us in the Americas today, learn history from texts in which 96% of the content speaks of the achievements of males?

Millions of women in our world have never heard the gospel or been taught to pray. If, or when they learn, will the gospel bring sight to the blind? Will it proclaim liberty to captives? When they learn to pray, will they come to know a God in whose image they are created, a God who companions them in their lives and experience? Or will they hear of a God who lords it over them, keeping them in bondage and fear? A little girl at a Sunday Eucharist with the ordinary prayers of the Roman ritual hears over 60 male metaphors for God. God is like a lord and a father. God is "he" and "him". God is like a male. Males are like God. Females are invisible. Females are unnoticed, females are unimportant. Evangelization and prayer are not bringing sight to the blind and liberty to captives. They are reinforcing the blindness and captivity the girl is already experiencing in education and society.

At the United Nations Conference on Women in Copenhagen in 1980 a study by the International Labor Organization states that women provide two-thirds of the world's work hours, and produce 44% of the world's food. On the other hand, women only receive 10% of the world's income and own 1% of the world's property. Women hold only 10% of the seats on national legislatures. Women work silently while men speak.

In the reform of the Liturgy of the Hours following Vatican II, on some of the feasts of women saints, selections of their writings have been given for the readings. I have raised the question, "Before this reform have the words of women ever been a part of the formal liturgy of the Catholic Church, whether for Eucharist, other sacraments, or Liturgy of the Hours?" I have consulted a number of liturgical scholars who balk at the question. They have not been able to give any instances of a woman's words and of prayer being used in the formal written rituals before Vatican II. In the Liturgy of the Hours, women might read the scripture and the prayers written by men. (Fragments of scripture may have been women's words and stories, but they are traditionally credited to males.) Women might add petitions for specific needs at specified places. The alleged words of Paul, "The voice of a woman should not be heard in the church," seem to have been interpreted to mean that women's words and prayers were never to be consulted for praying in the formal liturgy.

Lex orandi, lex credendi is an ancient tradition in the church. "The law of prayer is the law of belief." The way we pray determines what we believe and what we do. Since the people had prayed to Mary assumed into heaven over the centuries, this ground-swell of prayer was considered the basis for the institutional church's proclamation of belief in such an idea. Can a change in prayer lead to a change in belief and practice?

The Council of Trent wrote that if scripture and worship were translated into vernacular language, there would be great dangers of errors and the unity of truth and faith could be destroyed. Pope Pius XII in 1947 in "Mediator Dei", an encyclical on worship, repeated the same argument. Yet during the 1930's, 1940's, and 1950's, vernacular languages were being used in many liturgies in Germany, France, Austria, and Switzerland. These experiments provided information for Vatican II. It is imperative that we as women speak and test our words of prayer.

At the Last Supper, Peter was upset when Jesus wanted to wash the disciples' feet. Peter had not minded when Jesus healed people, fed them or did other things. Footwashing confused hierarchical structure, it confused masters and servants. Is hierarchy necessary for order and unity, or can hierarchy be replaced by a "discipleship of equals"? Our world needs new paradigms of power. "Power with" rather than "power over" is needed in the Christian community. Worship such as these services, can be one means of communicating new paradigms of power.

In biblical culture, it was not unusual for servants to wash persons' feet and for wives to wash their husbands' feet. It continues to be more common for women to wash children, the sick, and the elderly, than for men to wash others. Women washing feet is not a "subversive" activity, as Jesus–a–man washing feet. Women washing feet can say much about tenderness and intimacy, but it does not usually reverse the roles of power as Jesus' action did. Women giving service does not usually reverse roles of power.

Women sharing their own experiences, telling their own stories, speaking their own prayers, and celebrating their own rituals reverse the roles of power as Jesus' action of footwashing did. This may change in the future, but today speech is for women as footwashing is for men. Do we dare speak our own prayers? What will Peter say?

Martha Ann Kirk, C.C.V.I.
Feast of Saints Perpetua and Felicity, 1987

PREFACE

The WOC book of liturgies is the expression of many women's yearnings to know, love and serve God. Through liturgy and ritual we women place ourselves in the presence of God; we ask for God's healing and transforming love; we acknowledge and praise God for being in our lives through simple times and sad times, at milestones and turning points, in our visioning and in our celebrations.

Liturgies in this collection were submitted by members of the Women's Ordination Conference. They were originally created for prayer services or regular meetings of local groups across the country.

Why a collection of liturgies? This publication has been a long time coming and there are several reasons for the project. Through the WOC book of liturgies, WOC will continue to create a global linkage unifying women through prayer; nurturing the spirit of reconciliation among women and among women and men; and demonstrating the vitality of women's prayer in the latter part of this century.

The liturgies included in this collection have been selected on the basis of their creativity and adaptablity, their potential for satisfying different needs, and their diversity. They are meant to be a starting point for those seeking new ways to express God's importance in their lives. Users should feel free to either use the liturgies presented, or to experiment, enhance,and improvise until they develop a form that meets their needs.

To the extent possible, the original music and readings have been listed. They are not always published in full because obtaining permission to reprint copyrighted material would have delayed publication indefinitely. Addresses for obtaining sources are given.

The WOC book of liturgies is neither the beginning nor the end of the creation of feminist liturgies. Women have always composed rituals and prayers as they needed them. This book, however, acknowledges the feminist spiritual movement in the latter part of the twentieth century. WOC encourages all women who have been seeking new ways to express the movement of the Spirit in themselves to continue to share with us their testimonies of the collective feminine consciousness present in our world now. As we are able, we shall present these compositions to our membership through NEW WOMEN/NEW CHURCH.

Fidelis McDonough,RSM

CELEBRATE SUMMER: A FAMILY SERVICE

MICKIE DEMPSEY

YES, TO WALK IN CREEK BEDS AMONG SHARP LITTLE STONES, WITH BARE FEET AND READY.

INTRODUCTION: Summer-time, more than any other, is a time to take off our shoes. With bare feet we can feel God's earth: the damp grass, the hot sand, the ocean's creeping wavelets. With our shoe-less feet we can touch God!

READER: Exodus 3:1-5

RESPONSE: To each of the following petitions, the response is :
"WE TAKE OFF OUR SHOES, O GOD!"
- To see you in a summer sunset . .
"WE TAKE OFF OUR SHOES, O GOD!"
- To taste you in a refreshing summer drink ...
"WE ...
- To hear you in the crashing waves . . .
"WE...
- To smell you in a campfire meal cooking .
"WE...
- To touch you in a cooling summer breeze
"WE...

REFLECTION: A selection from *Seasons of Your Heart* by Macrina Wiederkehr, OSB.

"When I was a child wading in the brook, I understood totally the needlessness of shoes. Shoes in a brook are only for the overcautious, for those who would not dare to risk a stubbed toe. But there is no way to go through life without stubbed toes. At least, there is no beautiful way — no holy way.

There comes a time in one's life when the only religious thing left to do is to take off your shoes.

Take off your shoes to celebrate
the creek bed
the good earth or
a God who wants to speak to you from a burning bush.

There are things in our lives that stand between us
and the holy.
Getting rid of these things can be like a call to
take off our shoes
Stripping ourselves of the unnecessary giving up false gods
unmasking ourselves
knocking down walls between ourselves and the holy
freeing ourselves from cluttter
waiting with patience
removing all blocks to God's action in our lives and,
yes, to walk in creek beds among sharp little stones, with bare
feet and ready."

LEADER: And now, as a sign of our faith in God's presence throughout our summer fun and work, let's take off our shoes. And then we will pray Jesus' prayer of sisterhood and brotherhood: "Our Father/Mother . . . " (or sing or play Joe Wise's, "Our Father, Our Mother.")

THE BLESSING CUP: Now pass the cup filled with lemonade or other summery beverage.

SEEKING THE PURE WATER
MYRIEL C. EYKAMP, BARBARA HARRINGTON AND ANNE DALEY

INTRODUCTION: This liturgy was prepared as the culmination of an entire day at which we explored the interrelationships among women, spirituality, and the arts.

SPREADING THE FLAME: (Participants are handed candles. A single candle is lit and the light passed along. Participants hold their lighted candles while the poem is read, and then they burn throughout the liturgy.)

READING: "The Burning House" by Emily Brown

The flame is no longer held within the chamber
It burns everywhere
We are on fire
Children everywhere
Seeking water that will heal
The holy water
That is clear

Water unpolluted
But everywhere there is dirt and dust
That has settled into and poisoned the streams
Deep, deep down in the earth
There is the pure water

The way is down
The old sources have become clogged
New wells are sought
And sounding bars, divining rods, of every kind
Are held over the sands of our time
In efforts to discern the new watering places

That might be there
Deep down
For us

I have met her
That one
Who holds a true divining rod
That one who is seeking pure water

"The Burning Bush," by Emily Brown in Well of Living Waters ed. by Rhoda Head et al. C.G. Jung Institute of Los Angeles, 10349 W. Pico Blvd., Los Angeles, CA 90064. © Copyright 1977. Reprinted by permission.

SONG: "The Rock Will Wear Away" by Meg Christian/Holly Near on LP *Face the Music* by Meg Christian. Olivia Records, Inc. 4400 Market Street, Oakland, CA 94608. © Copyright 1977.

RESPONSE: (At this time participants — pre-selected or spontaneous — are asked to share their reflections on the poem.)

NAMING THE WOMEN WE KNOW BY HEART: (Participants are invited to name women brought to heart by the poem and reflections.)

SEEKING NEW WELLS WHERE THERE IS PURE WATER: (Containers of water holding palms and flowers are at each corner of the room. While music is playing participants distribute the flowers and palms and use the water to bless one another.)

SONG: "There's Something About the Women," by Holly Near on *Imagine My Surprise.* Redwood Records, 6400 Hollis Street, #8 Emeryville, CA 94608. © Copyright 1987 by Hereford Music (same address).

DANCING: All dance freely to "Waterfall," by Chris Williamson in *Meg/Chris at Carnegie Hall: A Double Album.* Olivia Records, Inc. 4400 Market Street, Oakland, CA 94608. © Copyright 1975.

BENT OVER WOMAN
KAY O'NEIL PBVM AND MICHELLE MEYERS, PBVM

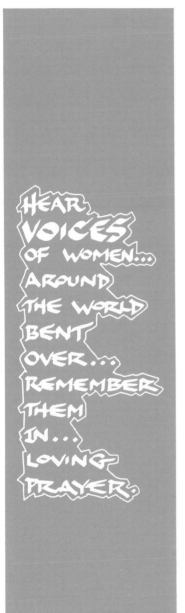

INTRODUCTION: The authors gathered with family and friends to celebrate a Silver Jubilee. They perceived this Jubilee Celebration as a means to celebrate the gifts of women amidst the sometimes overwhelmingly patriarchal church. As their Jubilee year progressed, the story of the Bent Over Woman took on more and more flesh as they shared it in a variety of ways with multitudes of wo/men. It became increasingly easy to develop "new forms" of telling the "Bent Over" story as they deeply internalized Jesus' message of freedom and hope amidst a church/world where we often feel powerless — from a male-only Vatican decision-making hierarchy to a government which seems deaf to cries of the people against nuclear arms buildup and invasions of other countries.

LITURGICAL RESPONDING: (Leader may be one or more persons.)

LEADER: (Tell the story of the Bent Over Woman, calling attention to the fact that this is a story of a bent over *person*, contrary to the usual way of dealing with women's passages in scripture, which identify this passage as "only" a passage for women. In telling the story, include:

- 18 years of infirmity - bent over (leader walks bent over in front of group, not able to see much, surely not self or neighbor when bent over.)

- She could not fully straighten herself, the power to change herself was out of her hands.

- Jesus saw her, called her and said," Woman (a term of respect, used for his Mother, Mary) you are freed from your infirmity."

- And Jesus laid his hands upon her. (Leader touches a person in front of the group.) Jesus was a "toucher" and healed through touch — "God's love with skin on" *versus* the abusive touches of pornography, incest, child abuse, rape, etc.

• And immediately she was made straight. (Leader stands up straight and walks around tall seeing self and neighbor.) Power of Jesus to transform people through touch/love of one another — "God's love with skin on" — you and me — the caring Christian community.

LEADER: Tells personal story of being Bent Over. (Leader's personal story models the depth of sharing for others.)

Leader invites the people gathered to turn to one another now and to tell their own stories of what bends them over, what keeps them from standing up straight and praising God and helping their neighbor. (Sharing time of 10-15 minutes in pairs.) Invite them to stand, to move around freely at this time.

Call the group back to their seats.

"Thank you my friends, for taking risks to share your own stories. Now I invite you to hear the voices of women from around the world who have been bent over by sexism, racism, poverty, ageism, alcoholism, militarism, etc. We hear these women speak, and we stand in solidarity with our sisters today. We remember them in our loving prayer."

READERS: From different places in the room, selected readers read brief testimonials. There is silence after the last reader.

Reader One: I experience loneliness, waste and sorrow when language ignores my existence and obscures the fullness of the risen Christ into whom all that is male and female is assumed.

Reader Two: I will graduate this spring with my Masters of Divinity. My male classmates will be ordained Catholic priests. Though I feel called by God to be a priest also, I can only hope for some position in the church.

Reader Three: I was married for 35 years. Six months ago, my husband left me to marry his secretary who is 25. Now because of the divorce settlement, I face the possibility of becoming one of this nation's elderly poor.

Reaer Four: I am an alcoholic. My Father was an alcoholic. I married a man who was the son of an alcoholic. When our son was a teenager, he permanently damaged his brain with "angel dust." I gave birth to another son whose father was not my husband. I don't live at home anymore — my husband has the children. I earn money for my meals and clothing as maid in the local hotels.

Reader Five: I came to —— as an undocumented worker whom your country calls an "illegal alien". My husband cannot find work. We eat food from trash cans. And now I am pregnant.

LEADER: Luke 13: 10-13

PRAYER: Either the leader offers a brief spontaneous prayer flowing from the experiences of the group and tying together concerns from testimonials, or participants may be invited to share their own spontaneous prayers with the leader summarizing and tying together.

SONG: "Small Bonfires," by Dorothy Davies
(See Appendix for musical score.)

Light the small bonfires my sisters
Set your spirits aflame
Bringing our message of freedom
We go forth in each other's name

REFRAIN: Whether you shout from the rooftops

or whether you speak quietly
Light the small bonfires my sisters
Till all God's people are free.

Loosen whatever may bind you.
Stand straight and know you are free.
Cast off whatever may blind you.
To things you do not wish to see.
REFRAIN

Do not let anger consume you
Use it, renewing the earth
Justice and peace are your vision
Strengthen yourselves for their birth.
REFRAIN

"Small Bonfires," by Dorothy Davies in Songs of Christian Feminism *and in* Songs of Womanspirit, *612 W. 11th., Willmar, MN 56201. © Copyright 1984. Reprinted by permission.*

Adaptations of the Bent Over Woman

Include time for people to share ways in which others have helped them not to be bent over, to stand up straight and praise God and to make a commitment to self and neighbor. This may be done as part of the opening prayer or later in the day as part of the closing prayer.

Use Marsie Silvestro's **"Blessing Song,"** to conclude a service on the Bent Over Woman, especially if people have shared together their own stories of pains, struggles, hopes. (See Appendix for musical score.)

Bless you my Sister
Bless you on your way
You have roads to roam before you're home
and winds to speak your name.
So go gently my Sister
Let courage be your song.
You have words to say in your own way
and stars to light your night.
And if ever you grow weary and your heart song has no refrain
Just remember we'll be waiting to raise you up again
And we'll bless you our Sister

Bless you on your way
And we'll welcome home all the life you've known,
And softly speak your name.
Oh we'll welcome home all the self you own,
And softly speak your name.

"Blessing Song," by Marsie Silvestro. Moonsong Productions, 2 Lee St., Somerville, MA 02145. © Copyright 1983 by Marsie Silvestro. Reprinted by permission.

Closing directions might be prefaced by some kind of a peace greeting/sharing/hugging time. This peace greeting may include an opportunity to tell others present how they have helped you to stand up straight, to praise God. Wish them the peace of Christ/ the love of God/the power to stand up straight.

Give people quiet time to write one way in which the world/ church will be challenged to wholeness/holiness because of their personal commitments to perform a certain deed by a given date. Part of the peace greeting time is used to share that commitment with another person who "receives" the commit- ment and gives a blessing of God's courage/power to stand up straight and carry out the commitment.

Use the WOC logo or another appropriate symbol/logo in some form as symbol of sisters standing together, standing straight, God's love empowering all through the concrete love of one another. These logos could be distributed in a myriad of ways left to the creativity of the participants in this service.

In closing, the group might gather in a circle —bent over— and through quiet reflection/peace greetings/"Small Bonfires" or "The Blessing Song" be led to a commitment to stand up straight, empowered by Jesus, in one another, to praise God and make a commitment to work for change in church and society.

THE WOMAN AT THE WELL
ROSE MARY MEYER, BVM

JESUS OUR LIBERATOR FREE US FROM FEAR AND MAKE US WHOLE WOMEN.

READING: John 4: 4-30

REFLECTION: In our Samaritan woman's meeting with Jesus, stereotypes are shattered. When Jesus' disciples returned from grocery shopping, they were amazed. The writer emphasizes, however, that the disciples knew better than to openly question and challenge Jesus' egalitarian practices. Not only was Jesus talking to a woman, but he was discussing theology with her! Jesus was deliberately breaking with rabbinic customs which were degrading to the self-concept of women. By his own practice Jesus showed us that traditions concerning men's behavior toward women did not always reflect God's intentions for humanity. Sometimes those traditions reflect cultural conditions which should be regenerated through the power of the Holy Spirit to bring new life to whatever has become fossilized. Obviously Jesus' actions of liberating acceptance had social consequences.

German writer Hanna Wolff calls Jesus "the integrated man"; in other words, a person who integrated and brought to maturity the masculine and feminine attitudes which are to be found in any human being.

All the Gospel writers portray Jesus as one who invited women to follow him. This Samaritan woman is but one example. Actually, she is part of the gradual movement toward faith that the writer of the Fourth Gospel portrays in Chapters 2, 3 and 4.

Jesus shares himself with her. She experiences Jesus and his revelation of God as a God of the earth, a nourishing and loving God. Jesus' dialogue with her brings her to wholeness rather than rejection, more brokennesss. Her thirst, her search to be liberated, a thirst every human being experiences, is satisfied. She came to carry water back to her home as have women for centuries. This time the water becomes freedom, like a river of life.

She becomes the first preacher to the Samaritans. She goes to tell the villagers the good news. Many believe her words. She sows the seed and waters it. She brings others to Jesus through her words. She proclaims and calls others to Jesus. This is discipleship.

RESPONSE: (All) Spirit of God, strengthen us in our search.

SHARED PRAYER: (As the group prefers).

THE WOMAN'S CREED:
I believe in God
who created woman and man in God's own image
who created the world
and gave both sexes
dominion over the earth.

I believe in Jesus
child of God
chosen of God
born of the woman Mary
who listened to women and liked them
who stayed in their homes
who discussed the Kingdom (kindom) with them
who was followed and financed
by women disciples.

I believe in Jesus
who discussed theology with a woman at a well
and confided first in her
his messiahship

who motivated her to go and tell
her great news to the city.

I believe in Jesus who
received anointing
from a woman at Simon's house
who rebuked the men guests who scorned her.

I believe in Jesus
who said this woman will be remembered
for what she did–
minister to Jesus.

I believe in Jesus who acted boldly
to reject the blood taboo
of ancient societies
by healing the audacious woman
who touched him.

I believe in Jesus who healed
a woman on the Sabbath
and made her straight
because she was
a human being.

I believe in Jesus
who spoke of God
as a woman seeking the lost coin
as a woman who swept
seeking the lost.

I believe in Jesus
who thought of pregnancy and birth
with reverence
not as a punishment–but
as wrenching event
a metaphor for transformation
born again
anguish–into-joy.

I believe in Jesus
who spoke of himself
as a mother hen
who would gather her chicks

under her wings.

I believe in Jesus who appeared
first to Mary Magdalene
who sent her with the bursting message
GO AND TELL...

I believe in the wholeness
of the Savior
in whom there is neither
Jew nor Greek
slave nor free
male nor female
For we are all one
in salvation.

I believe in the Holy Spirit*
as she moves over the waters
of creation
and over the earth.

I believe in the Holy Spirit as she yearns within us to
pray for those things
too deep for words.

I believe in the Holy Spirit
the woman spirit of God
who like a hen
created us
and gave us birth
and covers us
with her wings.

*The Hebrew word for Spirit is feminine.

"The Woman's Creed," in *Jesus and the Freed Woman* by Rachel Walberg. Paulist
Press, 997 MacArthur Blvd., Mahwah, NJ 07430. © Copyright 1986 by Paulist Press.
Reprinted by permission.

BLESSING: May God our Creator gift us as we continue the work
of establishing a world of peace and justice. May Jesus our
Liberator free us from fear and make us whole women. May the
Spirit enliven and enlighten us as we continue our discipleship.
Amen! Alleluia!

THE WOMEN'S ROSARY
LUCILLE MATOUSEK, SSND

JESUS... WHO LISTENED TO WOMEN AND LIKED THEM...

INTRODUCTION: To Catholics, May has traditionally been Mary's month. As children, and perhaps as adults, we have gathered together to pray the rosary, reminded of the joyful, sorrowful and glorious mysteries in the life of Jesus and his Mother, Mary.

Today these mysteries continue in the body of Jesus here on earth. Christ's body continues the rhythm of continous dyings and risings of the personal mystery.

As we see the body of Christ in its sufferings, we can continue to turn to Mary, model of faith, personal integrity, assertiveness, to be mother, sister and intercessor for us and for the world.

THE ROSARY
The Women's Rosary begins with the "The Woman's Creed" and the Our Father/Our Mother.

"The Woman's Creed" by Rachel Conrad Wahlberg (Complete text on page 25-27.)

ALL: I believe in God who created woman and man in God's own image
who created the world and gave both sexes dominion over the earth.

I believe in Jesus, child of God, chosen by God, born of the woman Mary
who listened to women and liked them
who was followed and financed by women disciples.

I believe in the Holy Spirit as she yearns within us
to pray for those things too deep for words.

Our Mother/Our Father

ALL: Our Mother, our Father, may your name be holy.
May your reign of justice and peace come,
May your will be done on earth as in heaven.
Our Father, our Mother, give us today our daily bread;
Forgive us our sin as we forgive those who sin against us.
Do not allow us to face temptation alone, but deliver us from evil.
For the reign of justice and peace, the power and the glory are yours,
Mother, Father, now and forever.

THE MYSTERIES: Each segment of the Women's Rosary includes 1) a reflection on a joyful, sorrowful or glorious mystery relevant to contemporary women; 2) recitation of "Dear Mary, full of grace...:. Samples of mysteries are given below:

A Sorrowful Mystery: Reflect on statistics of women in the labor force: education and wages. (Period of silence.)

ALL: Dear Mary, full of grace and faith,
God is with you!
You are blessed among women and men,
As is your child, Jesus.
Holy Mary, mother of God,
Pray for us, also your children,
Through every hour of our living and dying.
We ask in faith.

CONCLUSION : The song, "Bread and Roses," grew out of the 1912 mill strikes in Lawrence, Massachusetts. These mill workers, mostly women, fought to secure working conditions that would be physically safe and that would leave time for their spirits to thrive as well. These two values for which they struggled were symbolized by bread and roses.

We celebrate each day with the bread of our tears and the roses of our joy.

SONG: "Bread and Roses" by Mimi Farina and J. Oppenheim

As we come marching, marching in the beauty of the day
A million darkened kitchens a thousand mill lofts gray
Are touched with all the radiance that a sudden sun discloses
For the people hear us singing bread and roses, bread and roses.

As we come marching, marching, we battle too for men
For they are women's children and we mother them again
Our lives shall not be sweated from birth until life closes;
Hearts starve as well as bodies; give us bread, but give us roses.

As we come marching, marching, unnumbered women dead
Go crying through our singing their ancient cry for bread;
Small art and love and beauty their drudging spirits knew
Yes, it is bread we fight for, but we fight for roses too.

As we come marching, marching, standing straight and tall
The rising of the women means the rising of us all
No more the drudge and idler—ten that toil while one reposes
But a sharing of life's glories, bread and roses, bread and roses.

"Bread and Roses," by Mimi Farina and J. Oppenheim. (1912 Textile Workers' Strike Slogan)

Following the song, bread may be broken and shared among the group. Wine, apple juice, or other appropriate drink may also be shared.

Additional Suggestions for Mysteries:
Joyful Mysteries: Examples of reconciliation between women and men in the church. Positive changes in the churches' attitudes toward women. Women recapturing earlier liberating traditions.
Sorrowful Mysteries: Religious laws which discriminate against women. False accusations and misinformation which lead to further discrimination against women. Sexist language which causes discrimination.
Glorious Mysteries: Women who have been falsely accused, who have been vindicated by the truth.

LOVE'S FLAME

KAREN ETHELSDATTAR AND ANN DOEMLAND

TOUCHING THE MATCH, WAITING FOR... FLAME, I KNOW MYSELF LINKED TO EVERY WOMAN WHO HAS KEPT A HEARTH.

INTRODUCTION: This ritual is celebrated on the Sunday closest to February 2, or on February Eve, the first of the "cross-quarter days"; the greater Sabbaths which mark the high points between solstices and equinoxes.

THE RITUAL: The leader, or one of the participants, gives a brief explanation about the significance of this time (corresponding to the Gaelic Fire Festival. This feast of the flame, later called Candlemas, is the celebration in honor of Bridget, a.k.a. Bridge, Brigetis, formerly the White Goddess, the quickening Triple Muse. She was known as the Goddess of Poetry, Healing and Smithcraft. To St. Bridget were later attibuted some of her qualities.) Now at the high point between the Winter Solstice and the Spring Equinox, the fire of the old year is ceremoniously extinguished and the new fire kindled and blessed.

(Sage is burned for purification and sweetgrass for positive influence, an American Indian derivation.) This burned mixture is passed around for each woman to bathe in the smoke.

READING: "Chains of Fire," by Elsa Gidlow.

Each dawn, kneeling before my hearth
Placing stick, crossing stick

On dry eucalyptus bark
Now the larger boughs, the log
(With thanks to the tree for its life)
Touching the match, waiting for creeping flame,
I know myself linked by chains of fires
To every woman who has kept a hearth.

In the resinous smoke
I smell hut and castle and cave,
Mansion and hovel,
See in the shifting flame my mother
And grandmothers out over the world
Time through, back to the paleolithic
In rock shelters where flint struck first sparks
(Sparks aeons later alive on my hearth).
I see mothers, grandmothers back to beginnings,
Huddled beside holes in the earth
Of iglu, tipi, cabin,
Guarding the magic no other being has learned.
Awed, reverent, before the sacred fire
Sharing live coals with the tribe.

For no one owns or can own fire.
It lends itself.
Every hearth-keeper has known this.
Hearth-less, lighting one candle in the dark
We know it today.
Fire lends itself.
Serving our life.

"Chains of Fire," by Elsa Gidlow. Publication unknown; found in the newsletter of Womanspirit, an Oregon organization no longer in existence.

SHARING THE FIRE: (Each person has a candle.) The reader lights her candle and repeats the refrain, "Fire lends itself, Serving our life." Then she turns to the next woman in the circle, and gives her candlelight. This woman repeats the refrain and the movement continues around the circle.

The group of those appointed lights the torch, placed in the center, composed of four thin tapered candles bound together. Each person then places her candle in the holders provided.

REFLECTION: One of the participants speaks briefly on fire as purifier. She passes out blank papers and pens for each to write something she wants burned up/out or purified in herself. The bowl of ashes from the burned sage and sweetgrass is again passed around. Each woman in turn lights her paper and puts it in the bowl, saying as much or as little as she chooses to say about it. After each woman speaks, the group affirms, saying, "So be it."

THE CHANT: Each woman selects a thought for a refrain or choses a card with a refrain such as, "Fire-Desire," "Burn Rage," "Molten Center," "Love's Flame" etc. Each repeats her refrain individually, and then, holding hands in a circle, the group proceeds in a circle, each adding her chant layer by layer and again and again until the chant comes to an end in a natural way.

REFLECTION: One of the participants speaks briefly on fire as the center, fire as the molten center of the earth, as used in the baking and cooking of food, fire as the symbol of love, including mystical love.

The leader takes the torch from the center of the circle. She speaks briefly of what she wants to have at the center of herself, and then passes it around the circle, each woman doing the same. The group repeats, as each woman finishes, "And (Name) shall be well and all shall be well and all manner of things shall be well." (Taken from the writing of Dame Julian of Norwich.)

READING: (All stand). "Bakerwoman God," by Alla Renée Bozarth.

Bakerwoman God,
I am your living bread.
Strong, brown bakerwoman God,
I am your low, soft, and being-shaped loaf.
I am your rising
bread, well-kneaded
by some divine and knotty
pair of knuckles,
by your warm earth hands.
I am bread well-kneaded.

Put me in fire, Bakerwoman God,
put me in your own bright fire.

I am warm, warm, as you from fire.
I am white, and gold, soft and hard,
I am so warm from fire.

Break me, Bakerwoman God!
I am broken under your caring Word.
Drop me in your special juice in pieces.
Drop me in your blood.
Drunken me in the great red flood.
Self-giving chalice, swallow me.
My skin shines in the divine wine.
My face is cup-covered and I drown.

I fall up
in a red pool
in a gold world
where your warm
sunskin hand is there
to catch and hold me.
Bakerwoman God, remake me.

"Bakerwoman God," in Womanpriest: A Personal Odyssey by Alla Renée Bozarth. LuraMedia, 7060 Miramar Road, Suite 104, San Diego, CA, P.O. Box 261668, 92121.© Copyright 1978, 1988 by Alla Renée Bozarth. Reprinted by permission of the author.

CONCLUSION: (All reach together for the central torch, hold it up high, making a group blend of sound that feels right — a wordless sound coming from the center of each person. As the sound subsides, we put the torch back down.) Leader: "The circle is open, but unbroken."

SUPRISED BY THE SPIRIT
MARTHA ANN KIRK, CCVI

GOD IS FIRE... AND WHEN YOU HAVE LEARNED TO DANCE ON THIS FIRE, IT BECOMES COOL WATER

ARRANGEMENT AND MATERIALS: Semicircle seating focusing on an altar, candles, the Bible and red flowers. Nearby, but not visible, a tray of artistically arranged assorted bite-sized fruits and a basket containing one bottle of bubbles and a wand for each participant. Re-label the bottles "Holy Spirit Holders. 'Now you can keep her in her place.' Distributed by Your Daughters Shall Prophesy, Inc."

Clown with red clown nose and red and white costume.

Large signs that can be held up one at a time: "Fruit Distributor"; "Get your Holy Spirit Holder right here!"; "Now you can keep her in her place"; "Buy a holder for _____ ("those who know it all", "Bishops", "your own security" — whatever you'd like to say); "Clergy discounts available." (Signs and a Holy Spirit Holder are kept in a large bag.)

Two yard-long dowel sticks with long streamers of red and orange cloth attached.

GATHERING SONG: The author suggests part of "Ruah," by Coleen Fulmer. All are invited to participate in dance gestures of the chorus. (See Appendix for musical score.)

Ru-ah, Ru-ah, breath of God within us
Ru-ah, Ru-ah, Spirit of our God.

1. The Spirit of God within us crumbles the ancient walls, building a new creation, the city of God. REFRAIN

2. Have no fear within you, for I will be your strength.
The barren will be fruitful, the lame shall dance and leap. REFRAIN

3. Your power will come to full-ness in the weak and humble child, from the roots of the smallest flower to the hearts of the old and wise. REFRAIN

4. Old men will see their visions, young men will dream their dreams.
Women will be our prophets, with children in the lead. REFRAIN

5. A wisdom enfleshed in Jesus, grace that moves a new en-kindled in a people, the many and the few. REFRAIN

6. The Dance of all creation, Singer of living song,
Beauty from days eternal, the praise of a loving God. REFRAIN

7. Root of the stem of Jesse, tree with arms so strong, life that grows through dying, revealing a tender God. REFRAIN

8. The Blessed are strong, wise women, like Esther, Sarah, Ruth Bonding for generations in Spirit and in Truth. REFRAIN

9. The call goes out to nations for women to rise and stand birthing themselves in power, the meek shall possess the land. REFRAIN

10. We struggle as one for freedom our heart-beat,
the Spirit's song
Sisters in pain and gladness ancient our dance and strong. REFRAIN

"Ruah," by Colleen Fulmer on *Cry of Ramah*, cassette tape available from the Loretto Spirituality Network, 726 Calhoun, Albany, CA 94706. Also in *Celebrations of Biblical Woemn's Stories* by Martha Ann Kirk, CCVI. Sheed & Ward, 115 E. Armour Blvd., Kansas City, MO 64111. © Copyright 1987. Reprinted by perrmission.

OPENING PRAYER: (All stand)

First Minister: Let us pray for listening and laughing hearts. (Silence). Fill us with your Holy Spirit that we may learn to listen to your Word, to laugh and to delight in it, and to share it with others. This we pray in the name of Jesus who taught that the greatest folly is the greatest wisdom, Jesus who made death itself into a surprise of life, Amen. (Gestures for all to be seated.)

Second Minister/Number of Readers (if reading is divided into parts): Acts 2:1-21.

I. SEEKING THE FRUITS OF THE SPIRIT

The clown who has been hidden until now comes in carrying a basket of assorted fruits and hawking like a street vendor: "Get your fruit right here, freshest fruit in town, get your fruit here." She looks at all the people, says: "I'm Ms. Ruah, Fruit Distributor, best fruits you can get."
She walks among the people distributing fruit and improvising comments. Suggestions for comments:"Here's an apple for you, but remember what happended when they ate that apple in the garden."   "Have some grapes - oh you came because you thought you'd get wine in church — sorry, only grapes today." "Here's a kiwi for you and some avocado for you - I'm a multi-national fruit distributor!" "You can have this lemon. Hey, you say things are sour enough around here without any lemons?" "I've heard you are a Honey-Do. They all say 'Honey do this, Honey do that'. Here's a honeydew for you." etc.

Then the clown looks up suddenly as if she hears a voice from above, pauses, and says angrily: "What do you mean? These are the wrong fruits. I'm the Holy Spirit and these are the fruits I bring...What? Why are you always interrupting me? Why does it always have to be Father, Son and Holy.... Why don't you ever let me do anything by myself?... Okay, okay. I'll go check the book and see what the fruits are supposed to be."

She disgustedly goes and fumbles through the Bible, then sheepishly says to the "Voice": "Okay, I'll read it to them." Her voice changes to a tone of thoughtful care as she reads Galatians 5:22-25.

First Minister: Let us close our eyes and pray, (silence), Loving

God, how often we are confused seeking all sorts of fruits —
wealth, fame, power over... and not recognizing the very best
fruits that your Spirit has for us. Let us mention aloud or in the
depths of our hearts what fruits we need, what fruits our communities need..

While this time passes, the clown silently disappears and gets the
props for part two.

II. TRANSFORMED BY THE POWER OF THE SPIRIT

Second Minister: Luke 12:29, Jeremiah 20:9.

At the sound of bells or guitar music the clown enters slowly,
fearfully, as if walking on fire, with fire. She sweeps the sticks with
colored cloth in large gestures that look like leaping flames. The
improvised music or bell ringing should seem to build from a spark
to a roaring fire, and the clown dances faster and more power-
fully. Finally the dancer has forgotten fear and is caught up in the
beauty of the transforming flames. The dance comes to an end.
The clown reads or recites:"God is not cool water to be drunk for
refreshment. God is fire. You must not only walk on this fire, you
must dance. And when you have learned to dance on this fire, it
becomes cool water, but until you learn to dance — my Lord,
what struggle, what agony." Nikos Kazantzakis

Source unknown. Attributed to Nikos Kazantzakis

Clown disappears.

III. TRYING TO HOLD THE SPIRIT

Clown returns, carrying a large bag. Out of the bag she holds up
a sign and walks around the room with it. A person "planted" in
the audience reads: "`Get your Holy Spiirt holder right here'?
What's a Holy Spirit holder??" The clown takes each of the signs
and carries them around separately. The "plant" continues to
read them aloud trying to figure them out. The clown then puts
the last sign down.
She begins to mime breathing, then feeling a gentle breeze, then
a mighty wind. Suddenly she stops, points to her head as if she is
having an idea. She stands firmly with both arms out in a large
gesture and she starts to hold the air in between. Then she starts
to squeeze it together. This is extremely difficult. She strains and

strains until she's holding the air in a small ball in her two tightly cupped hands. Then she stops and with a big smile points to her head with another idea. Out of her bag she pulls a bottle marked "Holy Spirit Holder". She shows it to the "plant" in the audience who says: "Holy Spirit Holder?"

Then the clown happily opens it and begins blowing bubbles. She catches one in her hands the way she was holding the air before. She very carefuly takes this to the "plant" and gives it to her to be held in her tightly cupped hands. The "plant" indicates by word or smug gesture that she now has the Spirit held in her hands. The clown slowly begins to pry open the person's fingers and shows that there is no bubble left. She laughs and laughs.

The "plant" peeks into her hands. She is frustrated that the Spirit got away and she angrily stomps back to her seat.

First Minister: John 3:8

Loving God, your Spirit blows where she wills, sometimes soothing us with gentle breezes, sometimes devastating us like a tornado, sometimes filling our sails, other times knocking us over. Teach us not to be afraid, for your Spirit also gathers us into one body, a body that supports us when we are weak and consoles us when we are sorrowing. We know your gentle touch in the touch of others.

IV. THE CONSOLATION OF THE SPIRIT

Second Minister: God "will give you a comforter to be with you always: The spirit of Truth ... I will not leave you orphans." John 14:16-18

SONG RESPONSE: Suggested is "Gentle Loving God," from _Chants for Meditation_ by Rufino Zaragoza, OFM Conv., Credence Cassettes, NCR Publishing Co., Inc. 115 E. Armour Blvd., P.O. Box 414291, Kansas City, MO 64141. Published 1983.

First Minister: Let us gather in a circle, hold hands and chant together, "Gentle Loving God, the mother of my soul, hold me as your own." (or whatever song response is selected.)

As the chant is softly intoned, the clown goes around the outside of the circle, like a mother bird hovering over, gently touching with outstretched arms the shoulders of all in the circle.

V. THANKSGIVING AND BLESSING

Ministers: Bring the plate of fruit to the table in the middle of the circle.

Third Minister: Loving God, your creation reflects your beauty. We know you in the sweetness of flowers, in the touch of caring hands, in the color of fire, in the movement of dance, in the taste of fruit. You made all and said that it was good, very very good. Though people turned from you again and again, you never abandoned us. Spring always followed winter. The grain that falls into the ground and dies brings forth new life. Through the power of your Spirit, transform us into a people who can recognize you always and everywhere, in the fruits of the earth, in spiritual fruits, in the transforming fire of diversity, in the breath of life, and in the tempest of struggle. Bless this fruit. Bless us. Bless all who hunger and thirst, may we hear their cries and share the abundance you have given us.

First Minister: (Holds up the fruit) You are invited to take three or four diffferent kinds of fruit and to be seated. Then take time to look at each one, to smell it and slowly savor its taste. God gives us so much diversity and so much beauty in creation, so many precious fruits and gifts. Will we take time to recognize them and savor them? (As the fruit is selected and eaten, meditative instrumental music is played.)

CLOSING PRAYER: (one of the ministers can invite the participants to share closing prayers, and/or invite them to rise as this prayer is said.)
Let us pray with grateful hearts: (silence). Loving God, like a mother bird hovering over her young, you both shelter us from harm and teach us to fly freely. Like a clown, you interrupt and upset us, yet you amaze and delight us. You satisfy our hunger with the fruits of the earth and yet give us an insatiable longing for your banquet. May we live in the paradoxes and dance freely with your spirit. This we pray in the name of Jesus who taught us how to be foolish and who lives forever and ever. Amen

CLOSING SONG: "Ruah," from *Cry of Ramah* songs by Coleen Fulmer, dances by Martha Ann Kirk CCVI. (See p. 35-36.) All start to sing and dance "Ruah". Then suddenly the clown brings out the bottles of Holy Spirit Holders and hands them to people telling them to blow bubbles and pass them on. The song should continue long enough for a cloud of bubbles to fill the room.

CELEBRATION OF BEING IN THE MIDDLE OF THINGS

MARY ANN MCGIVERN

WE CRY OUT TO THE LIVING GOD: COME LIVE AMONG US.

INTRODUCTION: This is a celebration of being in the middle of things: a 25th anniversary. Twenty-five years doesn't seem very long at all. It is a point, though, of reflection. We eat and drink and sing and dance and be merry, not because we're finished or even in a particularly good place, but because sometimes it is good just to stop and say,"This is where we are," and to rejoice together over our very existence.

SONG: "How can I Keep from Singing," Shaker Hymn. public domain.

My life flows on in endless song above earth's lamentation.
I hear the real and endless hymn that hails a new creation.
Above the tumult and the strife I hear its music ringing.
It sounds an echo in my soul. How can we keep from singing?

When tyrants tremble, sick with fear, to hear their death knell ringing;
When friends rejoice, both far and near, How can we keep from singing?
In prison cells and dungeons vile, our hearts to them are winging.
When friends by shame are undefiled, How can we keep from singing?

What though the tempest loudly roars, we know the truth, it liveth.
What though the darkness round us grows, songs in the night it giveth.
No storm can shake our inmost calm, while to this rock we're clinging.
When love is lord of heaven and earth, How can we keep from singing?

REFLECTION: by Celebrants or Celebrants and participants

SONG: "Bread and Roses," by (See page 30)

PETITIONS: Individual prayers of petition may be offered here. The response is, "WE CRY OUT TO THE LIVING GOD, COME LIVE AMONG US."

OFFERING OF RICE CAKES, WONDER BREAD, TORTILLAS, FRESH BAKED BREAD, SWEET BREAD AND WINE.

RESPONSE: We offer bread and wine to God and to each other. We offer ourselves to God by giving ourselves to one another. May this offering of our lives be accepted by God. Let us each, in union with God and with one another, accept our gift in God's name and offer in God the gift of peace.

EXCHANGE OF PEACE: (When this time of sharing is complete, all gather in a circle.)

SONG: "Old Devil Time," by Pete Seeger. © Copyright 1969, 1970. Fall River Music, Inc., and Sigma Productions, Inc.

RESPONSE OF THE COMMUNITY: We thank you God for your gifts, We know who you are by these gifts: wheat and grapes and trees and bricks for houses and our friends who give us strength.

We remember the women and men who have lived and died in you: Jesus who was born in a stable and died on the cross; Gandhi who clung with his whole being to the knowledge that killing is wrong; Dorothy Day who knew it would be foolish to live anything less than what she believed (others, famous and unknown may be mentioned here who have gone on before us in the way of truth and love.)

Celebrants: The bread and wine are holy because we have blessed them with our lives. So let us break bread together and drink wine in memory of all those who live and die in God. (Instrumental music is played as the bread and wine are shared.)

FINAL BLESSING

CLOSING SONG AND DANCE

BUT HAVING SEEN YOUR FACE, WE WILL LIVE AND KNOW GOD HEARS.

WHO WOULD BELIEVE?

KERRY MALONEY

INTRODUCTION: This is a liturgy of commission, representing an effort to bring together a spirit of thanksgiving and celebration at a time that has potential to be painful and troublesome for a Catholic woman, with a remembrance and honoring of "unrecognized" apostles whose testimonies were doubted and whose authenticity was questioned. Among these Paul, who needed to defend his equality with the Jerusalem apostles in his own time, figures prominently. As a symbol of the shared leadership and religious authority with which we sent forth our friend, and as a testimony of her witness to the world, we gave her the cup and plate from which we drank and ate during the liturgy.

OPENING PRAYER: (Together) You have turned our mourning to dancing, dear God. There is great cause to rejoice!

(One person then prays spontaneously or uses a short reflective passage to set the tone of the liturgy.)

FIRST READING: Galatians 1:11-24.

SECOND READING: Luke 24:9-12

THIRD READING: Gospel of Mary, 18-19:

"When Mary had said this, she fell silent, since it was to this point that the Savior had spoken with her. But Andrew answered and said,'Say what you wish to say about what she has said. I at least do not believe that the Savior said this. For certainly these teachings are strange ideas.' Peter answered and spoke concerning these same things. He questioned them about the Savior: 'Did he really speak privately with a woman and not openly to us? Are we to turn about and all listen to her? Did he prefer her to us?'

Then Mary wept and said to Peter,'My brother Peter, what do you think? Do you think I thought this up myself in my heart, or that I am lying about the Savior?'

Levi answered and said to Peter,'Peter, you have always been hot-tempered. Now I see you contending against the woman like the adversaries. But if the Savior made her worthy, who are you indeed to reject her? Surely the Savior knows her very well. That is why he loved her more than us. Rather, let us be ashamed and put on perfection and separate as he commanded us and preach the gospel, not laying down any other rule or other law beyond what the the Savior said'...And they began to go forth to proclaim and to preach."

Excerpt from The Nag Hammadi Library in English edited by James M. Robinson. Copyright © 1978 by E.J. Brill. Reprinted by permission of Harper & Row, Publishers, Inc.

COMMUNAL REMEMBRANCE: (The gifts of the woman being celebrated are remembered here. At this time, participants call upon their collective and individual knowledge of the woman to be comissioned, to share reflections on her particular gifts and on her ministerial strength. Symbols for these gifts might include, for example, a cup of oil to symbolize healing, etc.)

POEM: "For Hagar and Other Women Who Sit Unwittingly Beside Living Water (Genesis 16)," by Kerry Maloney

Shaken out like the pleats of an ancient skirt,
my womb is the gateway of wanderings.
Fury and scorn, this slavery of sorrows
and no honor gained in a son's annunciation —
I am the handmaid of the Lord,
the handmaid of the Lord.

By wellsprings, I have been found.
Still, I am discovered there.
Hearing words of rebuke and gladness —
He told me all I have ever done.
Can this be he?
Can this be he?

Who would believe what I have seen?
(Who would really care?)
"The Lord has given heed to my affliction."
This child of exalted father will not be slain on altars of faith or
principle.

But having seen your face, we will live
and know
God hears.
Ishmael.

BLESSING OF WATER: Creator Spirit, you hovered over the chaotic
waters at the beginning of time to bring peace, order and life out
of tumult. Through the waters of the flood, parting sea, baptism
and Jesus' wound, you recreated and delivered your people. Be
present again as we bless this water, water in which we are
nourished before birth, by which we are cleansed and refreshed,
with which we spill tears in sorrow and delight. Loving Mother,
bring us newness of life and purpose through this water. We
praise you for this simple gift which sustains us, and we thank you
for your presence in its unending flow.

(The water is poured into a bowl and a cup from a pitcher.)

BLESSING OF THE WOMAN: (Each participant washes her hands in
the newly blessed water in the bowl before encircling the woman
who is to be commissioned for apostolic service. When the circle
is formed, the participants impose their hands — as one— on the
woman's head and pray silently for her.)

SHARING OF BREAD AND WATER: We have received the blessing
of (N's) friendship and her ministry. We have celebrated God's
choice of her to be the bearer of Good News by blessing her. Let
us now share this living water from the cup of blessing and this

bread among ourselves as friends. This simple meal, bread and water, is transformed from a symbol of austerity and punishment to a sign of celebration and a foretaste of the celestial banquet by our feasting together today on God's goodness in her gift of (N) to us.

ALL: (After the feast.) You have turned our mourning to dancing, dear God. There is great cause to rejoice!

THE COMMISSION: "(N), hear these words. "Tend the flock of God that is your charge, not by constraint but willingly, not for shameful gain but eagerly, not as domineering over those in your charge but being an example to the flock." (1 Peter 5:2-4)

NAMING CEREMONY: FOR A NEWBORN CHILD
BARBARA A. CULLOM AND DIANN NEU

BLESSED IS SHE WHO REDEEMS AND LOVES. BLESSED IS HER NAME.

GATHERING SONG: The authors used "Womanriver Flowing On," in album, _Womanriver Flowing On_ by Carole Etzler. Sisters Unlimited, Inc., 1492-F Willow Lake Dr., Atlanta GA 30329. © Copyright 1977.

CALL TO WORSHIP: Parents or others speak on the meaning and significance of the names chosen for this child.

READING: Excerpt from _The Story of My Life_ by Margaret Anna Cusack. London: Hodder and Stoughton, 1981.

"How little we can foresee the destiny of the newborn babe. Responsibility for the care of the little being who may be the work of so much good, or so much evil, is something to make the wise think more seriously. It is only the wise who fear, the foolish virgins never thought — anytime would do for getting oil for their lamps, but the wise are always ready because they are wise. Oh Mothers, who look on your newborn babe and fondly trace the likeness to the dear father or the dear mother or sister or friend, think, I pray you, of the other likeness — the likeness of God. It is for you to preserve that likeness, it is for you to see that the blessed relationship is understood when your little one is capable of understanding it."

READING: "On Children," from *The Prophet* by Kahlil Gibran. Alfred A. Knopf, Inc., New York, NY © Copyright 1972.

SONG: The authors used "Womanchild," by Carole Etzler. "Womanchild," in album, *Womannriver Flowing On* by Carole Etzler. Sisters Unlimited, Inc., 1492-F Willow Lake Dr., Atlanta, GA 30329. © Copyright 1977.

INVITATION TO SHARE: (Particpantrs were invited to reflect on how we all pass on life, not simply biological or adoptive parents, but God/ess parents, friends, etc. As each one shared, she lit a votive candle from one of two candles which had burned at the child's parent's wedding service.)

SAGE BLESSING: A home-grown herb is burned now to incense the child and parents. The following poem by an unknown author is read.

The Morning Water Woman is like Mother Earth.
She is Mother of all.
From her bosom came the water.
She gave all her children the plants and various species of animals from the tiniest ant to the biggest elephant and eagle.
The woman who nurses a baby is just like Mother Earth, giving to it so that it will go out into the world strong and steady.
When the woman brings in the morning water, she asks God's blessings on all, that everyone who drinks it, the good and the bad, that they drink it because they are her children.
She prays for everyone who is going to drink the water, first in the meeting and then in the whole world.
God gave her the privilege to pray for everyone, no matter where they are at, in conflict or at peace.
Anyone who drinks the water will remember where it comes from.
The woman is the symbol of Mother Earth.
They call her the Morning Water Woman and she is mother of all.
If your mother is gone, she is just like your mother.
Or, if your mother is still living, you have a second mother.
You came from a mother and to a mother you shall return.

BLESSING: This Blessing is attributed to Jonowitz and Wenig.

Blessed is She who spoke and the world became.
Blessed is She who in the beginning gave birth.

Blessed is She who says and performs.
Blessed is She who declares and fulfills.
Blessed is She whose womb covers the earth.
Blessed is She whose womb protects all creatures.
Blessed is She who nourished those who are in awe of Her.
Blessed is She who lives forever.
Blessed is She who redeems and loves.
Blessed is Her Name.
(All present are then invited to touch and bless the child.)

CLOSING SONG: "Blessing Song," by Marsie Silvestro.
(See page 22-23 for words to music. See Appendix for musical score.)

IN SEARCH OF MYSELF
KAREN ETHELSDATTAR AND ANN DOEMLAND

BEFORE HER... BEHIND HER, IT IS BLESSED... WITH LONG LIFE AND EVER-LASTING BEAUTY.

The following items will be used during the ceremony: an assortment of necklaces, bracelets, etc. Shawls are provided. Each person choses one or two of these at the beginning to be used later in the ceremony. (Also ready is a special jewel or precious stone, scented oil, three rolls of different colored crepe paper.)

INTRODUCTION: (A circle is formed. The convenor begins...) Let us begin by each anointing the woman to her left in the circle on the forehead, the throat pulse and the palms saying:
"Blessed be
all that you think
all that you feel
all that you do."

READING: "I am the sea..." (pp.147-150) In _Daughters of Copper Woman_ by Anne Cameron, Press Gang Publishers, 603 Powell St., Vancouver, B.C. VOA 1H2 CANADA. © Copyright 1981.
     (The reading is done sequentially, divided among those present. During the last section of the poem, "Old Woman is watching...", one reader continues while the rest of the group chants as a background, "Weave and mend, weave and mend..." All read the conclusion together.)

MEDITATION: "Let us ask ourselves in the quiet, 'What do I want to find in myself? Do I want strength? Do I want gentleness? Do I want fire? Do I want peace?'"
Time is allowed for reflection

Each woman in the circle will then share briefly what she has come up with, ending by turning it into her chant: "I am strong...strength is coming to me" (echoed by the group). As each woman shares in this way, she holds the special stone in her hand.

READING: "The Mother of Change presides over the making of Humankind...it is precisely her 'skin', her earth, corn, shells, obsidian, animal flesh, waters which imbue us with our variety and our own potential for transformation. Her substance goes into us." The legend says, "After some period of time, a child was heard crying for four days. The people would not find the child. They were afraid. First Man finally succeeded in finding a mysterious girl baby.' Below her stretched a Dawn Cord from the East and from the south a Sky Blue Cord, from the west a Twilight Cord and from the north a Cord of Turquoise. The child was rocking on Dawn and Turquoise rainbows, supported by these cords.' First Man recognized that Darkness was her mother and Dawn her father, and when he took her in his arms he found a small White Wind in her right ear and a small Dark Wind in her left ear, placed there by her parents. She was Changing Woman....She grew up in four days, reached maturity and wisdom in twelve days, and the Blessing Rite was given for her."

From A Magic Dwells: A Poetic and Psychological Study of the Navaho Emergence Myth by Sheila Moon. Guild for Psychological Studies, 2230 Devisadero St., San Francisco, CA 94115. Reprinted by permission.

LEADER: One of the Navaho transformation ceremonies, for ushering the pubescent girl into society and involving positive blessings on her, includes a ritual of adornment. We will use the necklaces and shawls selected earlier to decorate one another. This ritual of adornment is both a pleasure in itself and a symbol of our own changing.

READING: "She is decorated with soft fabrics,
now she is dressing her up.
She is decorated with jewels,
now she is dressing her up.

Before her, it is blessed; now she is dressing her up,
Behind her, it is blessed; now she is dressing her up,
Now with long life and everlasting beauty,
now she is dressing her up."

"Navaho Blessing Way Ceremonies," in *Seasons of Woman: Song, Poetry, Ritual, Prayer, Myth, Story* by Penelope Washbourn. Harper & Row, 10 East 53rd St., New York, NY 10022 © Copyright 1977. Reprinted by permission.

LEADER: Pick up my necklace — dress me with (*strength*.) (Hand necklace to dresser, who is the woman on your right.)

DRESSER: (Adorning her.) I dress you with (*strength*).

ALL: Now she is dressing her up.

DRESSER: Adds a blessing of her own. This blessing is echoed by the group. Continue around the circle until all women are "dressed".

WEAVING THE WEB: Sitting in a circle, the participants begin tossing rolls of different colored crepe paper to each other, forming a web that weaves around them and weaves them together.

READING: "Song of the Sky Loom"

Oh our Mother the Earth, oh our Father the Sky,
Your children are we, and with tired backs
We bring you the gifts that you love.

Then weave for us a garment of brightness;
May the warp be the white light of morning,
May the weft be the red light of evening,
May the fringes be the falling rain,
May the border be the standing rainbow.
Thus weave for us a garment of brightness. That we may walk
fittingly where birds sing,
That we may walk fittingly where grass is green,
Oh our Mather the Earth, oh our Father the Sky.

"Songs of the Tewa", trans. Dr. Herbert Joseph Spindeen in *Four Winds, Poems from*

(The group breaks the crepe paper to extricate themselves from the web, its remnants hanging as decorations about their shoulders.)

LEADER: We may go our separate ways, but our lives are interwoven. The circle is open but unbroken.

THE SPIRIT OF GOD IS UPON ME: TO PROCLAIM LIBERTY TO CAPTIVES

LYNNE SCHMIDT AND SSND FRIENDS

TO DO JUSTICE, TO WALK HUMBLY, AND TO BE COMPASSIONATE IN THE NAME OF OUR GOD.

INTRODUCTION: (Begin with participants sitting in a circle. In the center is a table with a candle.)

LEADER: Why have we gathered in this place?

ALL: We come in praise of the God of all life and in affirmation of Jesus Christ as the truth and center of our lives. We celebrate places where love is found in life, and we give thanks for the gift of new life that comes to us this day.

LEADER: Let us recall together our commitment to respond to the violence in our lives.

ALL: We commit ourselves to respond to the violence of dominating power and aggressiveness which leaves so many persons powerless and hopeless in their struggle for human dignity and wholeness of life. We call ourselves
• to expand our experiences and broaden our awareness of this force of violence in order to better understand and diminish its root causes,
• to confront dominating power and aggressiveness within ourselves, our communities, and those with whom and to whom we minister,

• to promote mutuality and collaboration in all our relationships, and
• to foster life-giving rather than life-denying forces.
(One person comes forward and lights the candle.)

READING: Jeremiah 1:2-10

RESPONSE: Psalm 139 (or appropriate song)

READING: Luke 4:18-19

REFLECTION:
Leader: Recall an incident in which you have experienced violence in the church or society within the past month. (Pause)
Reflect on what you learned from that experience (Pause)
What action has been or could be taken in response to the incident? (Pause)
(Those who wish to are invited to share their reflections.)

PRAYER: (One of those present calls the group to prayer).
Let us pause now in prayer for guidance in choosing an appropriate response to a specific form of violence in our lives.

READING: Selections from *Compassionate and Free* by Marianne Katoppo

Human liberation often seems to be a grim and joyless struggle. The Magnificat shows otherwise. And I exult in the fact that this Asian woman, this Mary, upon her encounter with God bursts out into this great song of thanksgiving and joy given to God, who liberates through the oppressed themselves. Through Mary, women in some special way personify the oppressed, although she represents all oppressed people, not just women.

Mary is the truly liberated, fully liberated human being: compassionate and free.

From Compassionate and Free by Marianne Katoppo. Orbis Books, Maryknoll, NY 10545. © Copyright 1980. Reprinted by permission.

MAGNIFICAT: (A familiar form of the Canticle may be used or all sing "Blessed is She," another form of the Magnificat.)

"Blessed is She" by Colleen Fulmer
(See Appendix for musical score.)

REFRAIN: Blessed is She, who believed that the promise made her by our God would be fulfilled, would be fulfilled.

1. And Mary said:
"Let me sing the praise of God
for having touched this lowly one
and from now on I shall be called:
'Woman most highly blessed."

2. Holy is our God!
whose kindness never ends
who by great strength
has scattered the proud
and raises up the poor
and gathers them into all fullness.

3. For God has come
to this servant Israel
to show all mercy
now and forever
as was promised Sarah and Abraham
and their children forever."

"Blessed is She," by Colleen Fulmer on Cry of Ramah, cassette tape available from the Loretto Spirituality Network, 725 Calhoun, Albany, CA 94706. Also in Celebrations of Biblical Women's Stories by Martha Ann Kirk, CCVI. Sheed and Ward, 115 E. Armour Blvd., Kansas City, MO © Copyright 1987. Reprinted by permission.

ALL: O God, give bread to those who are hungry and the hunger of justice to those who have bread.

BLESSING: (All stand in a circle with arms extended in blessing):
In your hearts, let there be generosity as large as the sea which accepts both clean and unclean waters.
So may you accept and cherish all as persons before God.
Let your hearts be as merciful as nature which loves the smallest tree or blade of grass, and as open to all people as nature to the heavens.

Let your mind be strong with sincerity that can pierce the iron and stone, so that you may be wise in your decisions.

Work always for the good of humanity in all its complex forms and expressions; be not closed to any human.

Make yourself above all, a person whom nature is pleased to let live.

Ancient Japanese blessing, source unknown.

CLOSING PRAYER: (One of those present calls the group to prayer)
Let us depart, filled with strength to do justice, to walk humbly, and to be compassionate in the name of our God.

THE COMING OF THE SPIRIT–
SHE EMPOWERS US ALL

MARGARET ARNOLD, EILEEN O'BRIEN MERCHANT,
FRANCE WHITE, SSJ AND JUDITH VAUGHAN, CSJ

WE, THE SISTERS OF GOD, SAY TODAY... ALL SHALL EAT... AND BE FILLED FOR THE BREAD IS RISING!

INTRODUCTION: This liturgy was celebrated on Pentecost Sunday, 1986, in St. Vibiana's Cathedral in Los Angeles by Los Angeles National Assembly of Religious Women (NARW)

WELCOME: We celebrate the coming of the Spirit.
(Response: She empowers us all.)
We are laywomen and members of religious communities who come together to work for justice in the church and in society. The Spirit calls us in. She calls some to the fulness of priesthood. Why does the church lock us out? We celebrate the coming of the Spirit.
(Response: She empowers us all.)

LITANY OF DELIVERANCE: (The response is "Spirit be freed and deliver us.")
From sexism and bigotry: RESPONSE
From heresy and inequality: R
From witch-hunts and name calling: R
From condescension and caste systems: R
From hierarchy and clericalism: R
From exclusion and institutional blindness: R
From threats and prohibitions: R
From rigidity and manipulation: R
From ignorance and fear: R

From misogyny and hostility: R
From deceit and lies: R
From unjust wage structures: R
From domination, alienation and subordination: R

(Incense is now lit, and slips of paper with the oppressions named above are burned with it.)

THE FREEING OF THE SPIRIT: As we burn these oppressions, we each light a candle and place it on the table symbolizing the freeing of the Spirit and the empowering of us all.

READING: "Call" by Alla Renée Bozarth

There is a new sound
of roaring voices in the deep
and light-shattered rushes in the heavens.
The mountains are coming alive,
the fire-kindled mountains
moving again to reshape the earth.
It is we sleeping women,
waking up in a darkened world,
cutting the chains
from off our bodies with our teeth,
stretching our lives over the slow earth,
seeing, moving, breathing in the vigor
that commands us to make all things new.

It has been said that while the women sleep
the earth shall sleep. But listen!
We are waking up and rising,
and soon our sister will know her strength.
The earth-moving day is here.
We women wake to move in fire.
The earth shall be remade.

"Call," from Womanpriest: A Personal Odyssey by Alla Renee Bozarth. LuraMedia, 7060 Miramar Road, Suite 104, San Diego, CA, P.O. Box 261668, 92121. © Copyright 1978, 1988 by Alla Renee Bozarth. Reprinted by permission of the author.

LITANY OF REMEMBRANCE: (Alternating sides)

I. As we prepare for our blessing and sharing of bread and wine, the central acts of remembrance of Christian faith, let us remember women who have allowed the Spirit to work through them. And in remembering them, let us invite them to be with us, that we might learn from their example.

II Saint Therese of the Child Jesus

I Convenors of the First Women's Ordination Conference of 1975

II All women called to renewed priestly ministry

ALL: Stand here with us!

I Fannie Lou Hamer and Rosa Parks

II Winnie Mandela

I All women who refuse to let racism be the law of the land.

ALL: Stand here with us!

I Theresa Kane

II Mothers of the Heroes and Martyrs of Nicaragua

I All women who proclaim the truth

ALL: Stand here with us!

(Litany continues as the group wishes)

BLESSING OF BREAD AND WINE: (Adapted from "Litany" by Carter Heyward)

ALL: We, the sisters of God, say today,
All shall eat of the bread,
And the power,
We say today,
All shall have power
And Bread.
Today we say,
Let there be bread.
And let there be power!
Let us eat of the bread and power!
And all will be filled
For the bread is rising!

READER: By the power of God
By the women of God
By the bread of God
By the power of bread
The power of women
The power of God
The earth is blessed
(The bread is shared)

ALL: Women are blessed
The bread is blessed
The power is blessed

The people are blessed
And the bread is rising

ALL: In the earth was the seed

WOMEN ARE BLESSED... BREAD IS BLESSED... POWER IS BLESSED

In the seed was the grape
In the grape was the harvest
In the harvest was the wine
In the wine was the power

We the sisters of God, say today,
All shall drink of the wine,
And the power.
(The wine is shared.)

"Blessing the Bread: A Litany," In Our Passion for Justice by Carter Heyward. The Pilgrim Press, 132 West 31 Street, New York, New York 10011. © Copyright 1984. Reprinted by permission.

SONG: "Song of the Soul," by Chris Williamson. *Meg/Chris at Carnegie Hall. A Double Album.* Olivia Records, Inc. 4400 Market Street, Oakland, CA 94608. © Copyright 1975.

CLOSING: LITANY OF CELEBRATION: (The response is: "Spirit, you have empowered us.")

For solidarity and cooperation,
For perseverance and courage,
For intelligence and competence,
For faith and vision,
For hope and love,
For unity and diversity,
For laughter and tears,
For anger and outrage,
For mystery and awe,
For listening and understanding,
For truthtelling,
For peace-making,
For mothering,
For tenacity and resistance.

THE HOPE WE SHARE
ROSE MARY MEYER, BVM

HOPE IS DEEP WITHIN US AND CALLS US NOT TO "WAIT AND SEE" BUT TO GO AND DO...

CALL TO WORSHIP: In the name of our Creator, our Liberator, and Sophia-Spiirt, we meet together this evening in hope and antici-pation that each of us will experience a journey that is liberating and life-giving.

MUSIC: A song which all know, or instrumental music to provide a bridge into the next section.

READING: "Women as the *ekklesia* of God have a continuous history that can claim women in Judaism, as well as in the Jesus and early Christian movements, as its roots and beginnings. This history of women as the people of God must be exposed as a history of oppression as well as a history of conversion and libera-tion. ...women of the past and the present...have acted and still act in the power of the life-giving Sophia-Spirit."

From p. 350 of <u>In Memory of Her</u> *by Elisabeth Schüssler Fiorenza. © Copyright 1983 by the author. Reprinted by permission of The Crossroad Publishing Company, 370 Lexington Ave., New York, NY 10017.*

MUSIC: Music should provide a reflective mood.

LEADER: Reflecting on the stories of past and presnt women nourishes us in the advent spirit of hope. In the midst of our journey — our exile, our slavery, our liberation — we hear the gospel call to justice and freedom and peace. We become the sacraments of God's life, the life-givers, holding out the ever-present hope of covenantal support, compassion, challenge in sisterhood. Hope is deep within us and calls us not to "wait and see" but to "go and do" — to be liberated. We envision a different future and different relationships.

SILENT REFLECTION

LEADER: As Celie in _The Color Purple_ grew from her experience of dehumanization, our image of God changes as our spirituality evolves. We reject cultic practice that dehumanizes and we experience the presence and the power of God's wholeness in EVERY human being.

Let us reflect now on our own history and recall to mind a human being who was life-giving for us — who revealed for us the presence of God and called us to wholeness, to liberation.

SILENT REFLECTION

NAMING THE NAMES: Let us now name those human beings who have been for us life-giving and liberating.
(Time is given for the naming and affirmation of life-giving persons who are present at this liturgy.)

CALL TO SHARE: Women — past and present —on our journey, let us now participate as our sisters have done for centuries in festive table sharing, the breaking of the bread and the sharing of the juice of grapes. We share this bread and juice of grapes in memory of our sisters through ages past, present and to come as life-giving symbols of wholeness.

SHARING OF BREAD AND JUICE: All share.

CLOSING ACCLAMATION: At evey moment of our existence, you are present to us, Creator God. We too are present to one another. May your presence be a sacrament of hope as we continue our journey toward wholeness, toward sisterhood of all. Amen. Alleluia.

MUSIC: (This may be a closing song sung by all or a composition which conveys the spirit of the acclamation.)

CELEBRATING THE DISCIPLESHIP OF EQUALS

EILEEN T. MCMAHON and
The Women of Long Island WOC

FORM A LARGE CIRCLE WITH LIGHT IN THE CENTER

INTRODUCTION: This ritual was celebrated at an Awards Dinner on the eve of the Ides of March.

PART I. Ceremony of Light (Let us stand in the presence of God.)

LEADER: Praised are you, Adonai, our God, Who have sanctified our lives through your commandments, commanding us to kindle the festive light. (lights candles.)

ALL: Praised are you, Adonai, our God, for giving us life, for sustaining us and for enabling us to celebrate this festival.

READER: As God called our ancestors out of the slavery of Egypt, God continues to call us out of our un-freedoms.

ALL: Praised are you, Adonai, our God, for giving us life, for sustaining us and for enabling us to celebrate this festival.

LEADER: Now let us form a large circle, with the light in the center.

READER: In the days of your prophet Deborah, You instructed Israel through the wisdom of a woman.

ALL: We stand together in union with Deborah.

READER: In the days of the faithful widow Judith, You saved Israel by the hands of a woman.
ALL: We stand together in union with Judith.

READER: In the days of beautiful Esther, You restored hope to Israel by the deeds of a woman.
ALL: We stand together in union with Esther.

READER: In the days of our beloved Ruth, You renewed Israel by the words of a woman.
ALL: We stand together in union with Ruth.

READER: In the days when the people of Judea were oppressed, in the reign of King Herod, in the town of Nazareth there was a faithful woman named Miriam.
ALL: We are ready, with faithful Miriam, to walk hand in hand with our faithful God.

MUSIC: The authors suggest the hymn, "Gather Us In", by Marty Haugen. © Copyright 1982 by G.I.A. Publications, Inc., Chicagi, Il 60638. From the book and recording, Gather Us In.

Verse 1 is used as an interlude. Verse 2 accompanies a procession to another room for Part II of the service.

PART II. Sharing of Wine and Matzoh

MUSIC: The authors used verse 3 of 'Gather Us In."

READINGS: Isaiah 51:1-5, 11-16
Excerpts from In Memory of Her, chapter IV.

(In Memory of Her by Elizabeth Schüssler Fiorenza. © Copyright 1983 by the author. The Crossroad Publishing Company, 370 Lexington Ave., New York, NY 10017.)

LEADER: On this night of bonding and community, we gather together to recall and celebrate God's promise of redemption to all people, to review our historic heritage, ratify our commitment and reflect on our personal responsibility to call others to discipleship. In recognition of the fulfillment of God's promise through Jesus and that we are God's disciples, we partake of the cup of wine.

ALL: (All drink of the wine.) Praised are you, Yahweh, Ruler of the Universe, who creates the fruit of the vine.

LEADER: This is the bread of affliction which our ancestors ate in the land of exile. All who are hungry, let them enter and eat. All who are unfree, let them come and join with us in our hope for freedom and equality.

ALL: Yahweh, our God and God of our ancestors, just as you took the Israelites from the land of exile and led them through the sea, so may You have mercy on all who are oppressed. Save them. Lead them from narrow straits to abundant favor, from darkness to light, from enslavement to redemption, now and forever. Amen. (All eat a portion of the matzoh.)

ALL: Praised are you, Yahweh, Ruler of the universe who brings forth bread from the earth.

PART III. Ceremony of Blessing.

MUSIC: The authors used verse 4 of *"Gather Us In"*

LEADER: Blessed are You, our Creator, our Friend, our Sanctifier, for calling us to celebrate this feast of freedom of the discipleship of equals.

ALL: You are oaks of justice that I have planted to show my glory. In every generation, I call my people. You know my voice. You yourselves shall be named priests of God. You shall call yourselves "ministers of our God." I your God, love what is right. I hate robbery and injustice. I will give you your recompense faithfully, a lasting covenant I make with you.

READER: Rejoice heartily in God, the joy of your soul. God has clothed you with a robe of salvation and wrapped you in a mantle of justice.

ALL: As the earth brings forth its plants and a garden makes its growth spring up, so I will make justice and praise spring up before all nations.

READER: The response is: Steadfast is God's kindness toward us. The fidelity of our God endures forever.

Praise to our God for life, for love of the earth, and for all therein.
ALL: RESPONSE

READER: Praise to our God for calling us to move from centuries old systems of oppression to the freedom of being the daughters and sons of God.
ALL: RESPONSE

READER: Praise to our God, ever-close to the poor and downtrodden of every age, God-with-us
ALL: RESPONSE

READER: Praise to our God who lights the way from passivity to activity, from dependence to autonomy, from isolation to community.
ALL: RESPONSE

READER: Praise our God for giving each of us the grace and courage to move from bondage to bonding.
ALL: RESPONSE

READER: Praise our God for giving us companions on our journey who are different yet who are one in their faith in you.
ALL: RESPONSE

READER: Praise to our God for the hope that the next generation will be free at last one day if we make the vision of equality a reality in our lives and in our world.
ALL: RESPONSE

ALL: In the day of distress, you called upon me and I set you free. I am with you. Fear not.
READER: What can anyone do against me? God is with me to help me. My strength and my courage is God, my savior. I shall not die, but live and declare God's works.

ALL: "Open to us the gates of justice."
ALL: Open to us all of the ministries to which you call your followers.

READER: "The stone which the builders rejected has become the cornerstone."

ALL: Women are rejected and do not experience the freedom in your church that, as your disciples should be theirs. Build your discipleship of equals.

READER: Make this a reality so we can say, "By God has this been done. It is wonderful in our eyes."

ALL: God has called us to leave the familiar, to journey through the wilderness. We have been given light, company and nourishment both materially and spiritually. The spirit of God is upon us. (Each person takes a turn blessing the person to her/his right as the following is read):

LEADER: God has anointed me
I have been sent to bring glad tidings to the lowly
to heal the brokenhearted
to proclaim liberty to the captives and release to the prisoners
to announce a year of favor from our God
and a day of vindication by our God
to comfort all who mourn; to place on those who mourn in Zion a diadem instead of ashes
to give them oil of gladness in place of mourning; a glorious mantle instead of a listless spirit.

Go in peace to the place where our God has given you responsibility. Go with the light of faith burning brightly, confident that God will nourish you in word and sacrament all the days of your life. Remember and teach our children that we are a people whose story is old but ever new. Our God will bless you, the Creator, the Son and Holy Spirit.

ALL: So be it! Let us incarnate the equality and the freedom of Jesus' disciples today and every day.

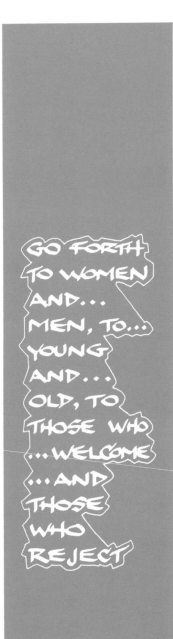

GO FORTH
TO WOMEN
AND...
MEN, TO...
YOUNG
AND...
OLD, TO
THOSE WHO
...WELCOME
...AND
THOSE
WHO
REJECT

EMPOWERING FOR MINISTRY
DIANN NEU AND BARBARA A. CULLOM

INTRODUCTION: This ritual was used as part of the closing ceremonies for the "Ordination Reconsidered" Conference in St. Louis, October 1985.

GATHERING: (All are invited to order space, weavings, vase and flowers, oil and napkins on tables.)
The convenor gathers up what the preceding days have been: she focuses on the goal of the ritual, "sending forth."

CALL TO PRAYER: "Spirit Movin'" by Colleen Fulmer

We're seein' how a mighty wind
Sweeps the surgin' waters
Spirit movin' where she will
Birthin' the light from darkness

REFRAIN
O Spirit Movin'
O Spirit Movin'
O Spirit Movin'
Movin' within your Daughters

We're seein' how creation breathes

Woven by this artist
Tapestries of pain and grace
Fire, flesh and stardust. REFRAIN

We're seein' how our sister-pain
Makes us strong in Wisdom
Broken Bread that feeds our world
Claimin' our faith and vision. REFRAIN

We're seein' how that Leaven grows
Long silent voices speakin'
Tellin' a story never told
The nations to justice leadin'. REFRAIN

We're seein a compassion born
The circle's growin' stronger
Lettin' our children live in peace
Copin' with wars no longer. REFRAIN

"Spirit Movin'" on album, <u>With Her Wings Unfurled</u> by Coleen Fulmer. Loretto Spirituality Network, 725 Calhoun, Albany, CA 94706. © Copyright 1989. Used with permission of the author.

INTRODUCTION TO READINGS: We have come to this place from many corners of the earth. We have spent these days together not always in harmony on method, but always in unity of spirit. Now, as we prepare to leave here. we listen to the words of empowerment our sisters around the world speak to us. Let their words, reflecting their commitments to stay in the struggle, inspire and strengthen us as Women-Church.
(Three symbols will represent each of the three readings. These symbols will be in the center of each table. At the invitation of each reader, one woman at each table will present the symbol.)

READING I: Julia Esquivel, exiled Guatemalan poet, uses the image of the weaver to convey the creative power of women. Let someone at your table unfold the weaving and put it in the center of your table to focus this poem. (Pause) Feel the weaving and listen to our Guatemalan sister, Julia.

"Indian Tapestry," by Julia Esquivel

When I go up to the HOUSE OF THE OLD WEAVER
I watch in admiration

at what comes forth from her mind:
a thousand designs being created
and not a single model from which to copy
the marvelous cloth
with which she will dress the companion of the True and Faithful
One.

Men always ask me
to give the name of the label,
to specify the maker of the design.
But the Weaver cannot be pinned down
by designs,
nor patterns.
All of her weavings are originals,
there are no repeated patterns.
Her mind is beyond
all foresight.
Her able hands do not accept patterns or models.
Whatever comes forth, comes forth,
but she who is will make it.

The colors of her threads
are firm: blood,
sweat,
perseverance,
tears,
struggle,
and hope.
Colors that do not fade
with time.

The children of the children
of our children
will recognize the seal
of the Old Weaver.
Maybe then
it will receive a name.
But as a model, it can never again be repeated.

Each morning I have seen how her fingers choose the threads
one by one.
Her loom makes no noise and men give it no importance,

None-the-less, the design that emerges from Her Mind
hour after hour will appear in the threads of many colors,
in figures and symbols which no one, ever again,
will be able to erase or un-do.

"Indian Tapestry," from Threatened With Resurrection by Julia Esquivel. © Copyright 1982 by Brethren Press, 1451 Dundee Ave., Elgin, IL 60120. Used with permission.

SONG: *Passionate God* by Colleen Fulmer (Sing verse 1 twice.)
(See Appendix for musical score.)

God is passionate life,
Strong and vibrant in us
as we seek   1. justice for all people
                    2. equality...
                    3. dignity...
                    4. peace in our day.

"Passionate God," by Colleen Fulmer on Cry of Ramah, cassette tape available from Loretto Spirituality Network, 725 Calhoun, Albany, CA 94706. Also in Celebrations of Biblical Women's Stories by Martha Ann Kirk, CCVI. Sheed & Ward, 115 E. Armour Blvd., Kansas City, MO 64111. © Copyright 1987. Reprinted by permission.

(Pause after song.)

READING II: Alice Walker, a Black American author, uses the image of her Mother's garden as a sign of women's commitment. Let someone at your table place the flower in the vase. Notice its shape and listen to your sister, Alice.

Excerpt from *In Search of Our Mother's Garden* by Alice Walker. Harcourt Brace Jovanovich, 465 S. Lincoln Dr., Troy, MO 63379. © Copyright 1984. pp. 241-242.

SONG: "Passionate God," by Colleen Fulmer. See above. (Authors recommend use of "vision in our lives" in the text) (Pause after song.)

READING III: Yosano Akiko, Japanese poet, reminds us that women are moving mountains. Smell the oil and awaken to the words of our sister, Yosano.

"Mountain Moving Day," by Yosano Akiko
The mountain moving day is coming
I say so yet others doubt it

Only awhile the mountain sleeps
In the past all mountains moved in fire
Yet you may not believe it
O man this alone believe
All sleeping women now awaken and move
All sleeping women now awaken and move.

"Mountain Moving Day," by Yosano Akiko. Found in Mountain Moving Day: An Anthology of Women's Poetry ed. by Elaine Goldman Gill. The Crossing Press, Box 640, Trumansburg, NY 14886.

SONG: "Passionate God," by Colleen Fulmer. (See page 73.) (Authors recommend use of "strength in our lives" in the text.)

REFLECTION: (by a guest or by the participants) (Pause)

SONG : "Blessed is She" by Colleen Fulmer (During this singing of the Magnificat there may be dancing.) (See Appendix for musical score.)

REFRAIN: Blessed is she who believed that the promise made her by our God would be fulfilled, would be fulfilled.

1. And Mary said: "Let me sing the praise of God for having touched this lowly one and from now on I shall be called: "woman most highly blessed."' REFRAIN

2. "Holy is our God! Whose kindness never ends, who by great strength has scattered the proud and raises up the poor and gathers them into all fulness." REFRAIN

3. "For God has come to this servant Israel to show all mercy now and forever as was promised Sara and Abraham and their children forever." REFRAIN

"Blessed is She" by Colleen Fulmer on Cry of Ramah, cassette tape available from Loretto Spirituality Network, 725 Calhoun, Albany, CA 94706. Also in Celebrations of Biblical Women's Stories by Martha Ann Kirk, CCVI. Sheed & Ward, 115 E. Armour Blvd., Kansas City, MO 64111. © Copyright 1987. Reprinted by permission.

COMMITMENT SHARING: At this time the participants are re-minded again of their purpose in coming to this conference. They are invited to share their personal commitments — what will they try to do when they get back home?

SONG: "Spirit Movin'," by Colleen Fulmer (See page 70-71.)

BLESSING OF OIL AND ANOINTING: Oil is a symbol of healing, of strength. We use it to anoint and bless, to empower us for our ministry. Take the oil on your table, bless it, and anoint one another.

COMMISSIONING: (This message will be spoken in several languages.)

(English) Sisters, go forth to all corners of the earth to bless and to heal, to sanctify and to celebrate.

(Spanish) Go forth to the hungry and the full, to those who sorrow and those who rejoice.

(Italian) Go forth to those who are wise, and to those in need of wisdom.

(French) Go forth to women and to men, to the young and to the old, to those who will welcome you and those who will reject you.

(English) Go forth in the name of the Creator God, the God/ess of Love, the God of the small and the powerless. Go forth to renew the earth!

(All languages together) Go forth and bless the world!

SONG: "Women are Rising," by Carolyn McDade. Surtsey Publishing, % Womancenter, 76 Everett Skinner Road, Plainville, MA 02762. © Copyright 1983.

THE PRESENCE OF
THE FEMININE GOD
LOUISE CUNHA

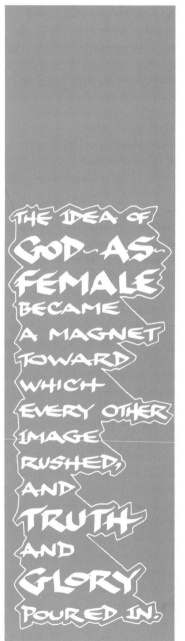

THE IDEA OF GOD AS FEMALE BECAME A MAGNET TOWARD WHICH EVERY OTHER IMAGE RUSHED, AND TRUTH AND GLORY POURED IN.

INTRODUCTION: Women often advocate inclusive God-language, but do we do this ourselves, in our own prayer life?

ALL: In the name of the Creator, and of the Sanctifier, and of the holy Spirit. Amen.

READER: Isaiah wrote: "Does a woman forget the baby at the breast, or fail to cherish the child of her womb? Yet even if these forget, I will never forget you." (Isaiah 49:15)

LEADER: Let us remember the presence of God the Creator as we place the Bible on the table.

READER: Julian of Norwich was an English mystic, somewhat unknown until recently, but now compared favorably to Catherine of Siena. In 1373, in the longer version of her book, *Showings,* she included a chapter on her vision of God as Mother. "As truly as God is a Father," she wrote, "as truly is God our Mother." She wrote of God as mothering us at birth and caring for us compassionately in life.

READER: Reta Finger, an editor and publisher of <u>*Daughters of Sarah*</u> writes:

"Suddenly the idea of God-as-female became a magnet toward which every other image rushed, and truth and glory poured in.
—The water of life swirled in a bathtub into which I climbed, and God herself got down on her knees to wash me clean of sin and guilt.
—I felt secure under the immense ferocity of a mother grizzly bear protecting me as her cub.
—I watched Bakerwoman God knead her bread. Those hands, gnarled and veined, were brown; and when my gaze moved upward I saw she was indeed a big, rugged Black woman."

"Fugue and Counterpoint," Editorial by Reta Finger in Daughters of Sarah. March/ April 1985,Reprinted by permission.

(Participants are invited to share images of God the Mother.)

READER: Matthew reported the words of Jesus, "Jerusalem, Jerusalem, you that kill the prophets and stone those who are sent to you! How often have I longed to gather your children as a hen gathers her chicks under her wings, and you refused." (Matthew 23:37-38)

LEADER: Let us remember the presence of God the Sanctifier as we place this cross on the table. (Use a picture of Christa, if possible.)

READER: Julian of Norwich called Christ, "our Mother, our Brother and our Savior."
(Participants are invited to share images of Christ as daughter.)

READER: Peg Donahue said that some people — like the early Hebrews —would have us think of the Spirit as feminine, since so often people do (wrongly) think of the Creator and Sanctifier as only masculine.

LEADER: Let us light this candle and remember the presence of God the Holy Spirit.

READER: Acts 2:1-4

READER: Reta Finger writes, "The Fire of God came down in tiny tongues over the scraggly twigs of an African woman cooking her children's supper in the twilight.
—From now on, when I wait upon the (Creator) to renew my

strength, the wings upon which I shall mount are those of the female eagle.

—And of course Wisdom, who was before all things and played and laughed with God at the dawn of creation — Wisdom took the shape of the loving and witty middle-aged woman who became my mentor and friend during my first job out of college."

"Fugue and Counterpoint," Editorial by Reta Finger in Daughters of Sarah. March/April 1985. PReprinted by permission.

(Participants are invited to share images of God the Holy Spirit.)

LEADER: Let us join hands and pray, as we may never have prayed before:

Our Mother, who is in heaven..."

ALL: In the name of the Mother, and of the Daughter and of the Sister Spirit. So Be It!

APPENDIX

SMALL BONFIRES
Words and Musoic by DOROTHY DAVIES

BLESSING SONG
Words and Music by MARSIE SILVESTRO

RUAH
Words and Music by COLLEEN FULMER

BLESSED IS SHE
Words and Music by COLLEEN FULMER

PASSIONATE GOD
Words and Music by COLLEEN FULMER

SMALL BONFIRES
Words and Music by DOROTHY DAVIES

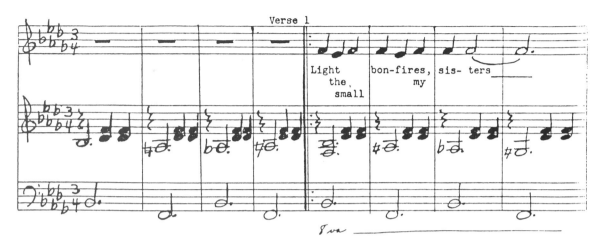

wheth-er you speak
qui-et-ly _____ Light bon-fires, sis- ters _____ Till
the my
small

|1.2.| |Last|

all God's peo-ple
are free. ___ free. _____

Verse 2
Loosen whatever may bind you
Stand straight and know you are free.
Cast off whatever may blind you
To things you do not wish to see. REFRAIN

Verse 3
Do not let anger consume you
Use it, renewing the earth.
Justice and peace are your vision
Strengthen yourselves for their birth. REFRAIN

Dorothy Davies

SONGS OF CHRISTIAN FEMINISM

BLESSING SONG
Words and Music by MARSIE SILVESTRO

RUAH
Words and Music by COLLEEN FULMER

Refrain:

Ru-ah,____ Ru-ah,___ breath of God with-in us___ Ru-ah,____

Ru-ah,___ Spir-it of our God.

1. The Spir-it of God with-in us crumbles the an-cient walls, building a new cre-a-tion, the ci-ty of our God. (to refrain)

2. Have no fear with-in you, for I will be your strength.____ The bar-ren will be fruit-ful,___ the la-me shall dance and leap.____ (to refrain)

3. Your po-wer will come to full-ness in the weak and hum-ble child, from the roots of the small-est flo-wer___ to the hearts of the old and wise.___ (to refrain)

8) The Bles-sed are strong, wise wo-men, like Es-ther, Sa-rah, Ruth___
Bond-ing for gen-er-a-tions in Spi-rit and in Truth.___ (to refrain)

9. The call goes out to na-tions for wo-men to rise and stand___
birth-ing them-selves in po-wer, the meek shall pos-sess the land. ___ (to refrain)

10. We strug-gle as one for free-dom our heart beat, the Spir-it's song.___
Sis-ters in pain and glad-ness an-cient our dance and strong. ___ (to refrain)

BLESSED IS SHE
Words and Music by COLLEEN FULMER

Refrain:

Blessed is she ___ who be-lieved ___ that the pro-mise ___ made her
by our God ___ would be ful-filled, ___ would be ful-filled. ___

1. And Mary ___ said: ___ "Let me sing the praise of God for having touched this lowly
one ___ and from now on I shall be called: 'woman most highly blessed.'"

2. "Holy is our God! ___ Whose kind-ness ne-ver ends, who by great strength has scattered the
proud ___ and raises ___ up the poor and ga-thers them in-to all full-ness." ___

3. "For God has come ___ to this servant Is-ra-el to show all mer-cy now and for-
e-ver ___ as was promised Sarah and Ab-ra-ham and their chil-dren for e-ver." ___

86

PASSIONATE GOD

Words and Music by COLLEEN FULMER

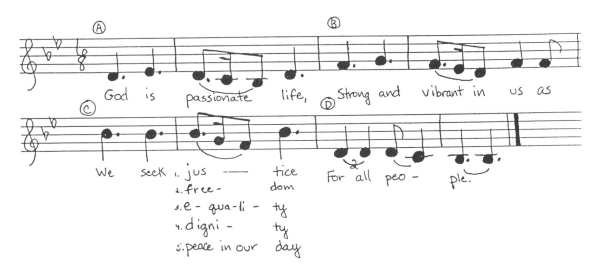

God is passionate life, Strong and vibrant in us as

We seek
1. jus —— tice
2. free- dom
3. e - qua-li - ty
4. digni - ty
5. peace in our day

For all peo - ple.

WOMEN'S ORDINATION CONFERENCE:
MEMBERSHIP INFORMATION

WHO WE ARE

The Women's Ordination Conference is an international grassroots movement of women and men committed to the ordination of Roman Catholic women—to a renewed priestly ministry.

WOC members are women and men who believe:

• the Church, in fidelity to its Gospel mission, must be equally open to the full participation of women and men in its ministries.

• women do image Jesus.

• women have an equal right with men to have a call to renewed priestly ministry respected and tested.

• oppression of one race by another, one class by another, one sex by another is not compatible with the Christian ideal of Church or priestly ministry.

• decisions affecting the life of the whole Church reflect female as well as male experience and thought.

WHY THE ORDINATION OF WOMEN?

As long as the Catholic Church excludes women from ordination:

• women participate only in a secondary, auxiliary way in the sacramental life and ministry of the Church.

- the Church fails to acknowledge the full effects of Baptism on women.

- women have no official role in the decision-making processes of the Church.

- the Church limits recognition of women as full persons, created in the image and likeness of God.

JOIN US

As a member of WOC, you join an international organization whose collective power:

* supports and develops a network of people struggling for the liberation of the oppressed, among whom are the women of our contemporary world and Church.

- seeks to recognize and authenticate women's gifts in the life of the Church.

- identifies women who feel called to a renewed priestly ministry.

- shares in Christian feminist efforts on every continent.

- lobbies for the removal of gender as a criterion for priestly ministry.

- reflects theologically on the experience of women in the Church.

- prays to be faithful to the liberating message of the Gospel.

- affirms what is priestly in each member of the Church.

- attends the annual National Conference of Catholic Bishops' meetings as press, representing WOC's newspaper, NEW WOMEN, NEW CHURCH.

- participates organizationally in the Women-Church Convergence movement, "a Discipleship of Equals."

WHAT CAN YOU EXPECT FROM WOC?

• NEW WOMEN/NEW CHURCH, a bi-monthly newspaper.

• workshops, seminars, conferences and think-tanks on local, regional and national levels.

• a clearinghouse of research and information. Media resource.

• assistance and support of local and regional groups. National Networking.

• dialogue with theologians and bishops.

• reclaiming of our history and reflection on women's story today to provide a new visibility for women.

• WOC members at important gatherings of the institutional Church.

• participation in coalition building with other feminist groups

• building base communities

• working for Church renewal and transformation of structures.

If you want to participate in a lively network of people who take these concerns seriously, JOIN WOC.

W.O.C. MEMBERSHIP FORM: NEW MEMBERS ONLY

(PLEASE DO NOT USE AS A RENEWAL FORM.)

Name _____

Address _____

City _____ State _____ Zip _____

Phone (day) _____

Phone (night) _____

Membership: ❑ New   ❑ Expired

❑ U.S.$25. regular USA membership
❑ U.S. $30.00. Overseas membership
❑ U.S. $10. low income/justice membership

Do you feel called to ordination?
❑ Yes ❑ No ❑ Not sure

((Please write checks or money orders on U.S. banks only.
WOC is incorporated as a 501 (c) (3) non-profit organization.))

I want to make an additional tax-deductible contribution:
❑ US $200 ❑ US $100 ❑ US $75. ❑ Other

Please return membership form to:
WOC Membership; P.O. Box 2693; Fairfax, VA 22031.
For more information, phone (703) 352-1006.

LIBERATING LITURGIES
Order Blank

Please send me _____ copies of Liberating Litugies
(Prepaid orders only.)
I enclose $8.50 for each book ordered.*   _____
$2.00 for postage and handling   _____
TOTAL   _____

Pre-paid bulk orders of five or more books cost $7.00 each plus postage/handling.
Call or write for more information.

Name _____

Address _____

City _____ State _____ Zip _____

Day Phone _____ Night Phone _____